# Contents:

| | |
|---|---|
| This Chapter Will Change Your Life Forever | 5-7 |
| How To Start Your Dreams Today | 8-13 |
| The Cause Of Your Results | 14-19 |
| Why People Keep Failing | 20-25 |
| Your First Step To Living With Purpose | 26-31 |
| The More You Give, The More You Get | 32-36 |
| How To Choose The Right Business | 37-43 |
| The Money Chapter | 44-48 |
| How To Brand Yourself | 49-51 |
| The Laws Of Success | 52-58 |
| Meet Jiri Majkus (My Story) | 59-62 |
| The Decision Making Process | 63-65 |
| Recommended Personal Development Products | 66-67 |
| Recommended Internet Marketing Tools | 68-69 |

# This Chapter Will Change Your Life Forever

Let´s talk about money. Everyone wants more, right? And I am going to tell you about three ways to earn it and keep earning more.

You owe it to yourself, your family and your society to earn more money. Good people get better when they are given a lot of money just as bad people become worse. Many people say that being a rich person is bad, that money is the root of evil. But this is another lie. Evil is the root of evil. Money is just a piece of paper, and with money you can do a lot of good, helpful things. I believe that you are a good person so I will reveal to you these money earning secrets that have radically changed the way I look at money.

If you follow the recommended strategies, you will earn an enormous amount of money. So here are three ways to earn money.

## 1) Trading time for money

The first way to earn money is by trading time for money. This way contains a lot of hard labor and in fact it is not really effective. Around 90% of the population sticks with this paradigm. But they are making only 5% of all the wealth in the world. Maybe it sounds crazy, but it is true.

"If I work hard, maybe someday I will get the good job." This habit we have from youth and it is deeply stored in our minds. But the problem is that if I am a factory worker, office worker in large company, lawyer or doctor I am restricted to time and if I want to earn more I need to work more. This situation is not pleasant because a day only has 24 hours and if I want to explode my income maybe I will not be able to do that because THERE IS NO TIME.

You literally trade your life for money. What a terrible thing to trade life for. Also if you are working for someone else, you are limited in your results. You build someone else's dreams not yours. There is always a limitation. Even though there are many people who will tell you that there is some security in working for a large company, that could not be further from the truth. How many people do you know that have been laid off or "reengineered" in the last 10 months? You see. The only security you have on this planet is within your own self.

## 2) Trading money for money

Next we have an excellent way to earn money. This is where you are trading money to earn money, or investing. This is great strategy but only in the case that you have the money, skills and proper courage. In this way there are big wins, big risk and also big loses. It is not very practical for the average person.

If you consider this strategy, I would strongly recommend you to get help from someone who really understands this topic, not someone who has only external experiences, but from who is already using this method and is successful in this strategy. Check his value, references, and results. When you do this check it again, just to be sure.

## 3) Multiplying your time through MSI´s

This strategy is the best way to earn money. Approximately 1% of the population uses this method and they make 95% of all the money that is being earned. That is right; one percent of the population earns over 95% of all the money. Don't you want to know what they know? Wouldn't be nice? If your answer is YES, let's look at the most powerful strategy.

It is when you multiple your time by setting up multiple sources of income (MSI). This is when you're leveraging your time through the efforts of other people and systems. You multiple your time, it is not how much you can do alone it is what you can do, systemize it and duplicate it. This is why it is so exciting.

The great thing about this strategy is that you are not having only one source of income, you have MANY. You see, when you want to explode your income you cannot do it just by working more, you have to work smarter. When you do this you will be absolutely blown away with what happens when money comes to you from different sources. When you do it properly, you are able to achieve income that you may have never imagined before.

### Take action now

Take action now by beginning to plan ahead, create a vision of exactly what you will do with the money when it comes and work on your personal development so you become a better person at the same time. Pablo Picasso said that "Action is the foundational key to success." Nothing happens only dreaming, there have to be an action.

Start doing and you will have whatever you want.

Set a goal, create your vision, contact me today and I will demonstrate to you how this strategy can work for you and how to become the person that you want to be right away.

# HOW TO START YOUR DREAMS TODAY

*Let's Talk About Your Results*

Looking at your present results will help determine if you are on the right track, because many people never stop to "take stock" of their results. They simply go through their life and never ask themselves the tough question that will really bring fulfillment and success their way. When you see your present results you can ask yourself a question: Is this what I want or I do I want to change something?

It is critically important to evaluate your results, because you can go a long time getting unwanted results while being very comfortable. Comfort will not bring you happiness, progress will bring you happiness. The nature of this world is that there is only progress or regress. Nothing like steadiness exists. The way to get progress is by first looking at where you are in your life.

Looking at your present results causes reflection and you reflect upon things, you learn a great deal. Reflecting is hard work, however, and not many people do it. But the ones, that do get great results. And when results comes, the inspiration reveals, from inspiration comes positive thought and only positive thoughts can create a better, opulent chapter of your life.

Wisdom comes from reflection. Everyone has experiences, but the ones who reflect upon the experience can get the realization how things works and from that point you can take control of your life.

Identifying where your results are can be very difficult, but it is very valuable, because to change your present results and get yourself where you want to be, you must first know where you are today.

*What Do You Value in Life?*

To me, values are the things, people, places and events that are most important to me in life. Every person has a different values and I have to at first find out what the values are for me, because values bring me the most fulfillment and joy. When I am not in harmony with my values, I am not happy and I feel like I am dying. The more in harmony my behavior is with my values, the more fulfilled and happy I am. This is a simple formula and it works for everyone.

Values are important, because when I know what is primary to me in my life I can set up my life in harmony with them, which brings me fulfillment. The important thing is to know what my values are, what these values mean to me and how they affect my life. Because the more I prioritize what I value, the more my life is filled with joy and gratitude. I will be talking about gratitude later, but it is the one of the best and powerful feelings you can experience.

When you are out of harmony with your values you will be unhappy and dissatisfied, because your priorities are not correct. You live how you do not want to live. You act contrary to your desire. You will always feel like you are missing something. You will always be chasing after something and never will be able to find it. This way of thinking can delay your happiness for quite a while.

When you do not live with your values you will regret and have to live with that regret your entire life. Now is time to set up your values. You cannot come back for a second try. Do not wait for success. The last thing I do not want to do is regret what I didn´t do that I should have done. If you are reading this and having regrets, remember this – IT IS NEVER TOO LATE TO BE WHAT YOU COULD HAVE BEEN!

Identifying your values brings you great joy, because if you have not identified your true values, how do you know for sure exactly what you value? When you do not live in harmony with your values, you live according to values of others and this cannot bring you happiness. This may seem like a hard question to answer and it can be hard for you, however, you cannot ask a question without already having the answer. This is designed to get you thinking.

You will have no regrets in life if you just answer this question at any point of decision: "What Would Love DO?" The answer to that question is always in alignment with your highest values. As long as you are answering that, you can do no wrong when you are in rapport with love. Operating in alignment with your highest values brings you the highest feelings of love imaginable. Love is the ultimate guiding emotion and love truly is the ultimate experience of all beings. Love never fails, love knows no boundaries and love is not the destination – love is the way.

You will be your best self at all times while in harmony with your values.

You identify your values by simply asking yourself what is important to you. How many people do you know take time out of their day to ask that simple, yet profound question? Not many I would assume, unless you hang around with successful people who are incredibly happy on a daily basis because it is those people who take time out of their day and ask themselves these questions. This is thinking. This is thinking about what is important to you and prioritizing your day accordingly.

What do you admire in others, those point out your values, because as you recognize what you admire in another personality, you are becoming aware of what you value most in life. If you admire someone, because they are very organized and that inspires you – then get to organizing your life in a hurry, because you value that quality. If you admire someone, because of the amount of time they spend with their family, then start making more time with your family, because you value that probably more than you are aware of. As you do this, you will find yourself truly happy. You will not be chasing your happiness around like the rest of the world, you will open your mind, heart and soul and embrace it within, because it has always been there waiting for you to just open the door!

What are your dreams, what is your desire, what do you want to do in life? These questions are the most important, because if you do not know what you want, you will never find out your values. And if you do not know what you want and what your values are, your life will be a big mess with no meaning, and no purpose. What do you really want? Ask yourself on a daily basis.

Open your mind and imagine how truly you want to live. Do you know that life is a movie and you are the director? It is you who choose the people, places and circumstances. It is you who choose the chapters and you choose what happens. Don't be an extra in your own movie. You can create your destiny, or your destiny will be assigned to you by external circumstances, other people, other desires and other values. The beauty is that we have a great gift and this gift is nothing else than freewill. You can control your results to an enormous extent. But nothing can become real to you unless you are aware that it is real. Use your ultimate power – power of choice.

Everyone starts with one step and the first step is usually the hardest for most people, but also the first step is the most important. When you take action the things start moving toward to you. You never figure out the best way to achieve your goal. In fact this is not your business. Your business is do things, hold your vision in mind with faith that you will get what you desire and let the universe take the rest. You will be amazed how things are arranged towards your goal. Remember that you have the vision and God arranges things toward you. When you realize this, you will be very grateful because you know that universe is friendly to you and you can have whatever you desire.

Every great goal first started out as impossible, but this might be just our point of view. In fact such a goal is exactly the way it should be. Most people are looking at their present results and they live according to what they think that they can do. But successful people first set up their goals, what they want in life, and after that they take action to achieve their goals. In the other words, you can live according to your present results or you live according to the results that you want to have.

Take the first step. That is all that is required and as you read through this book the first step that you must take will be revealed, keep reading.

You can make money doing anything you are passionate about and if every act you do is efficient. Every act is, in itself, either efficient or inefficient. To make each act efficient you have only to put power into it. And every act can be made strong and efficient by holding your vision while you are doing it, and putting the whole power of your faith and purpose into it. Do not forget that money is the materialization of a big, beautiful, service oriented idea. Money is ideas on paper – GREEN PAPER NOTHING MORE!!!

I will talk more about this in the Money chapter later on in this book.

## *Three Powerful Questions*

Who am I, what do I want, what is my purpose? If you would ask people for the answer to these questions almost nobody gives you a clear answer, nobody knows what to say. Often the answers are similar to this: I am Jack, I am this body, I am I, I want to enjoy, purpose does not exist, and life is just a chance. No one can tell you what you want and what your purpose is. Only you can find answers. And if you find them you will live a wonderful life.

Ask yourself who you are in order to learn about yourself, because when you deeply study this question, you discover that you are not this body. You are not bones, flash, blood and skin. Everyone says that this is my hand, not I am this hand. In fact you are spiritual living being, eternal energy with infinite power. With this understanding you cannot be ever dissatisfied.

Learning about yourself is extremely important, because everything in your life starts with you. You are the most important person in your life. You can be your own best friend. When you find the power and beauty inside you all this power and beauty will be expressed in your "outside" life. If you are not operating on this higher level, you cannot give anyone else the best.

As I have stated earlier, you must ask yourself what you really want to do with your life. You are the director of your life and if you do not take this control, someone else will. Other people, other circumstances will assign your destiny, either you or someone else. It is up to you, it is your choice what life you will live. If you have a clear vision and if you have this vision fixed in your mind, nothing can turn you away from your way to achieve your goals. I would recommend you again ask yourself what you really want on a daily basis. The more you ask the better you understand – the better you understand the more efficiently you do – the more efficiently you do the more you will have. Be, do and have – work on the being and the rest will take care of itself.

To find what you want in life, you must know what you are looking for. If you do not know what you are looking for, how you could know that you have found it? Most people run through life as fast as they can looking for "something". They really don't even know what, but they know whatever it is they don't have it and they must get it. It is only until it is too late to realize that what they were looking for was all around them.

I will be talking about purpose later, but your purpose is unique to you and only you can fulfill it. You have talents, skills and passions that no man or woman has ever taught you. Have you ever wondered why you are just naturally good at some things? These are all clues into your true life purpose – follow the synchronicity.

Only you can fulfill your purpose and your purpose is not something you "have to do". Meaning this – many people think it is their "slot" to live a life they don't like. They think their place in life has been setup for them and they need to suffer through it – this is not the case. Your purpose will be the most beautiful thing in your eyes. Your purpose is your why and you do it with love. It will bring out more passion and energy than you ever thought you could experience. It is just for you – your own unique present delivered from the universe right to YOU.

Your purpose is your why – it is your reason for being. Without a purpose people literally slowly disintegrate to death. Have you ever noticed when people retire they are filled with disease or even die shortly after – this happens to many people – why? Because without growth, comes disintegration.

## *Anyone Can Change Their Results?*

Absolutely YES! The sure way to fail is to not even try. This is not about taking a chance as much as it is GIVING you a chance. When you begin, you have already won the biggest battle in life – the battle between you and the fear of failure. When you can defeat that giant, you are well on your way. A major part of success is just showing up.

If one person did it, anyone can do it. Every single person has the same potential as anyone else. There is no more life in a mouse, than in a lion. There is no more potential in a person living in poverty, than a person living in abundance. Both have the same potential, both have the same gifts – one has simply opened them up and is PLAYING with them.

## *The Choice Is Yours*

Everyone fails; let the dead bury the dead. Never let yesterdays failures mar your vision of tomorrow. I have failed countless times, life has beaten me up time and time again but one thing I have mastered is getting back up. I never give up I will never surrender and I will never be outworked by anyone anywhere. If you put me and another person on a treadmill, I will win or die trying. If I can, you can too and I can show you the way.

You failed because you tried; trying is failure with a nicer name. There is no trying – only doing. There is no failing – only learning. There is no taking – only creating when you work with me.

# The Cause of Your Results

## The Definition of Attitude

Attitude is the composition of your thoughts, feelings and actions. It is important to understand that if we are talking about attitude, we cannot separate these three elements. Attitude is literally all of these elements together. When they are in harmony they form attitude and attitude brings results. Simple formulation is that if we have a good attitude it brings good results and when we have a bad attitude it brings bad results. So attitude is the primary cause of your results.

If you don't have a definition of what attitude is, you will find it hard to change it somehow. If you are not satisfied with your current results probably you should change your attitude. But when you do not know what attitude means and especially if you don't know what YOUR attitude is, it will be very difficult to change your results.

With deeper understanding, you will have more control of the goals you want to achieve. The more you understand what attitude is, the more control you will have over your attitude. Most people are not really aware of this fact that attitude is very important in our life because it directs your most powerful element and this powerful element is nothing else than your mind. When someone has his attitude out of control, his mind is also not really in harmony. With a disharmonic mind it will be very difficult to take control of your desired goals. So let´s build more of an understanding attitude so you can gain more control of your mind and in the end, your results as well.

The more you control your attitude; the better your life is. The more you control your thoughts, feelings and actions (attitude) the better you can predict your results. If your attitude is persistent and positive you will get amazing results in your life. It is just that simple.

## Attitude's Impact

In every area of your life, attitude has an impact because again, your attitude is the cause of your results. We can mention one of the universal laws, law of Cause and Effect. Cause is your attitude and results are the effects.

You choose your attitude no matter in which situation you are. The magic is to take control of your attitude under any circumstances. You have to be tireless in this case, if you know how to force your attitude towards your goals in any situation; you are the master of your mind. In fact when we deeply think about this, we can see that our reactions are mostly habits or we respond through our sub consciousness. You can choose if you want to change your habits in such a way that you will react in harmony with your goals.

It started to form when you were young, even if you were not aware of this. As an infant we have an open subconscious mind for any outside ideas and for any outside influences. So unconsciously we form our attitude according to other ideas. You could not stop the thoughts, feelings and actions of these things around you from going right into your subconscious and becoming fixed. Ask yourself what was the attitude of the people around you when you were an infant. Now realize that you are an extension of this energy up to some degree.

Authority figures in your life shaped and molded your attitude to an enormous degree. It is amazing when we stop and think about it. Now you can change your attitude according to your desire and I will show you exactly how to do it as you read further in this chapter.

Your own choices formed your attitude as well. Habits are results of our choices that we make consistently every day. Now every single morning, no matter what happened the day before, you can make a choice to set the attitude that you want to embody and hold that vibration during the day. The sooner you make this decision the better your days will be and your dreamed results will come very fast.

## Attitudes Impact on Family Life

If you have a positive attitude, your family will have a positive attitude towards you. This is natural principle of energy. Energy always come to the source and if we vibrate a positive energy, positive energy in the form of people, relationships, and circumstances will come back to us. If you have an attitude that you are very glad that you can spend time with your family, they have the attitude that they want to spend time with you too.

You will be able to communicate better and communication is the most vital aspect in any relationship. The better you can communicate the better the relationship you will have with your family. Every relationship will improve including your relationship with the outside world and with yourself.

A negative attitude from you causes a negative attitude toward you. Remember, with every feeling and action you are sending out a vibration that everyone around you can *feel,* whether they know it or not. I bet that at least once you were in situation that even you do not know why, you feel bad or good vibrations from some people. Unfortunately most people think about bad things and this has a definite impact in their family life. That's why in these days there are so many disappointed people because they have bad relations with their family. Right before you get home from work, decide to adjust your attitude accordingly and cultivate an attitude of gratitude that you have a family, they are all present and you have time to spend with them.

What you give out comes back, negative attitude from you, negative attitude towards you, positive attitude from you, positive attitude towards you. It is worth to repeat over and over again.

The better your emotions are, the better you communicate with your family. The better you communicate with them, the better relationship you will have. For sure you know what it is to speak with someone who has got a very bad mood. It is a hard to deal with, right? The more anger you are harboring, the more altered your perception becomes of your current reality.

You will have more fun together and that will perpetuate it and recreate more positive circumstances in your family life. It is a beautiful cycle and one that controlling your attitude on will have major benefits. The more you are grateful for the good times, the more good times you will have with your family. It does not get any simpler than that and it does not get any better than that.

## Attitudes Impact on Health

Your emotions affect your health significantly, more than you can imagine. Every emotion you have is like feeding your body with subtle food. The body reacts to subtle food the same way as it reacts on normal food. When diet is good, body has no problems to digest it, but when you eat some unhealthy food; your body will have a problem to digest. The same is with subtle food in form of your emotions.

The better your attitude is, the better you feel, the better you feel the more efficient your actions are and the better results will come. Start to heal your body through positive feelings and of course healthy diet. You will find your attitude instantly improves when you do this.

A negative attitude affects your immune system. It literally affects your liability to sickness and disease. Talk to a chiropractor or a healer and they will tell you that some of the main components of good health are proper movement, nutrition and positive thoughts.

When you get sick, you won't heal as fast. This may sound slightly incorrect, but there have been many studies done that have proven people with positive attitudes are convalescing faster and often demonstrate amazing results with their psychical healing.

You will be more susceptible to getting sick and you will find that your will leads you this way to be sick when you have these negative thoughts! Remember you literally become what you think. You rarely find someone in a constant negative state who is shiny and healthy!

The better your attitude is, the better you feel and when you feel good you spread a positive vibration which people can feel. You can easily say when someone is in a positive vibration by the way they walk, talk and sound. Your body instantly responds to your attitude and feelings.

You will discover that you will not get sick as often as you used to and when you do, you will not stay sick as long.

Pure thoughts cause you to not desire unhealthy food. It was James Allen who said that in his classic book "As A Man Thinketh": Great is that the more you feel good, the more you will desire to feel good and you will not want to put any toxic food into your body. When you are in such a state your mind itself will be looking for better feelings.

## Attitudes Impact on Social Life

Cause and effect. Emerson called the law of Cause and Effect the Law of Laws. This law works in every relationship. When you have positive thoughts you attracted positive people with positive circumstances. It is just that simple.

An attractive personality is someone with a positive attitude. Your thoughts, feeling and actions are in positive harmony and you become charming and magnetic. You spread positive vibrations and everyone is attracted by you, because it is very pleasant to be in the company of positive people. Their hearts are shining like a sun.

Have you ever talked to someone with a negative attitude? It probably was not very funny. It was probably very hard to communicate with him, because he acts with anger and anger changes the perception of the current reality. WHO WANTS TO TALK WITH SOMEONE LIKE THAT!!! Not me and I am sure you don't either.

People will not want to spend a lot of time with you if you are in a constant negative state. There exists some people, who want to be with you, and these people have the same negative mood and it will be very pleasant to complain with them that everything in this world is wrong. But these people are almost only talking about problems, they do not solve them. "Misery loves company" is a very true statement.

You will be magnetic and people will love to be in company with you because you spread only positive vibrations and they can feel these vibrations. There is no better cure for negative emotions than some positive impulse. Some joke, big smile or something like that. Sometimes people will tell you that you are like a healer for them.

People will want to be around you and STAY with you. You will find yourself developing great relationships that are both meaningful and profitable.

People will look for you to do business with. It can be also someone who you have never met before. There is no better marketing than your own attitude. You cannot buy these forms of marketing, because it is in YOU.

## Attitudes Impact on Financial Life

Everything goes with money. When you have a proper attitude money will come. It all starts with your attitude. Get out and get in massive action with the right thoughts, feelings and actions and you will find that money will find you and follow you.

If you have a negative attitude towards a friend, will he stay for a long time? The same rule is with money, if you have negative thought even if you suddenly acquire a large amount of money, probably you will spend them very fast or lose them. Why? Because you deserve just what you think what you should deserve. If you think you do not deserve any money you are telling the universe that you do not want any of them. And the universe says: "Your wish is my command."

Negative attitude equals poor service and poor service is not the key to wealth. You have to give service that is valuable for the others. In negative state you do not want to give anything to anybody.

Money will get away from you, escape you and it will be a constant source of frustration for you the more you will maintain these feelings and perpetuate a negative attitude towards it.

On the other side you will magnetize money and it will come to you more fluently because your actions will be consistent.

You will provide better service and better service is one of the aspects of the Law of Compensation which I will discuss later in chapter about earning money! You will want to stick around for that one!!

People will want to do business with you and they will literally seek you out, just like I stated earlier. This all sounds crazy until you experience it and then it gets even crazier!

## How to Improve Your Attitude

YES! It starts today! It starts the minute you decide it is going to improve. REMEMBER THIS: Every single morning you must come back to the decision and to the commitment that you are holding a positive attitude all day long no matter what. Lock into that vibration and the universe will reinvest to bring you good things it is pure unadulterated magic!

*Step 1:* Describe and write down to yourself the attitude you want, in every detail. When you are in circumstance where your attitude gets sidetracked – write exactly how you want your attitude to be relative to the circumstance in which you are.

*Step 2:* Read it every day. Every single morning and every single night as a reminder of the attitude you are holding.

*Step 3:* Get around the right people as soon as possible. Once you have decided you are changing your life, contact me NOW! I want to know and I want to connect you with right people, the right family and the right way which will take you from where you are now to where you want to be.

# WHY PEOPLE KEEP FAILING?

## *What belief actually is*

The belief is an idea which I am convicted about. This belief may have originated from some book that I read, from a strong experience I have or it can be just memory that I repeat over and over again in my mind. There is a difference between thinking the truth and believing the truth. The belief is something beyond that. The belief is something I know that I know.

The belief may be true or it may be totally incorrect. Just like as attitude can be positive or negative it is the same with belief. If I believe in negative things then the belief turns against me. When my belief is focused on positive things then big things start to happen. This can be a little confusing at the beginning but as you read through this chapter you will have a deeper understanding and you will be able to take appropriate action.

Learning about my beliefs and their power over my actions has completely changed my life. I can see many people trying to achieve their goals, but these goals are completely contrary to their belief system. For example, if you are trying to make more money, but your hidden belief's system is convinced that you are not worth the money, you never get it. You can try and try, but there is a simple truth that we attract only what is in harmony with our belief. You can do amazing things when you believe that you can do it and you deserve it. You have to turn your belief from negativity and start to believe that you are able to get what you are looking for. Let's start to set up your belief system in a positive way.

You can only change what you are consciously aware of. And our beliefs are contained in the subconscious mind and they stay there until we "go deeply inside" and start discovering what these beliefs really are. When we look at our beliefs we can consciously decide which beliefs are good for us and which are not. From that point we can transform our beliefs to a positive way.

## *How belief can be positive and negative*

Beliefs can be negative if they are not based on truth. Just because you believe in something it does not make it true. If I believe that when I jump from a building and nothing happens to me it does not mean that law of gravity will not work at that time. You can ask yourself a powerful question: Is that true, or is that what you believe? This question is very good when you realize a belief that needs changing.

If you believe you are a total failure your results will always be negative for you. You cannot have wonderful results when your mind is fixed, thanks to the belief system, on millions of reasons why you cannot achieve your goals. Focus only for a reasons why you will achieve your goals. This is very important – REMEMBER THAT.

If you believe you are not worthy of having a great bank account you will not have a big, juicy bank account because your belief system is not in harmony with what you want. When you occasionally get some amount of money, but if you believe that you do not deserve it, you will attract different circumstances, which will take the money from you. Maybe you have some experience with this. Everyone wants more money, but the main cause if you will actually have it is hidden in your inner belief system.

Beliefs can be tremendously positive if they are based on truth. And the truth is that you are a SPIRITUAL BEING with INFINITE potential. Anything can be done if you believe that you can do it. The universe is friendly to you so there is no reason to fail, if you have a positive strong belief. Believe in YOU and that universe will give you whatever you desire.

Beliefs are very good if they promote your potential and again your potential is unlimited, just like in any other man. Such potential that people can fly in a plane, travel to outer space, build beautiful buildings, overcome sport records and many other amazing things. You will rise only as far as your beliefs will let you – there are truly no limits. Absolutely none and you have to include this information with your beliefs system and your behavior.

Your beliefs will unlock your inner genius and I truly and completely believe that you are a genius. I may not know you, I may not know anything about you, but I know that every single person is a genius; he just has to be aware of it. We all have the same potential; there is no difference between the president of United States and the cleaner in any restaurant. NO ONE has more potential than anyone else. Just like my mentor helped to find hidden genius in myself, YOU can do that too and I will help you. I am very grateful that I know this powerful knowledge and I want to help others to unlock this beautiful experience and realization. Then you will truly discover that anything can be done. But if you do not follow what I am going to explain to you in this chapter,

## *How belief strengthens us*

Your motivation is based on your belief that you can do what you want. Why would you be motivated to do something you believe will end with failure?

When you wake up in the morning, if you believe bad things are going to happen you feel like you do not want to get up from bed. There is no motivation, no belief that today will be another great day in your life. Start to affirm that only positive and good things happen to you. Start thinking about your success. Take ownership of things you want before they actually come to you. How would you feel if your dream car was in the garage, if your account will be big and juicy and your perfect partner was sitting right next to you? How would you feel? These things make you feel good.

You will be much more committed if you believe that you will succeed, you will not hesitate to take action toward your goals. If your belief is strong, other people will feel that you are committed and you will inspire them, they will want to be in such a state too.

If you act with half-hearted action, you will eventually fail every single time. Put everything to every single action, which is toward your goals. Make every action like it was dedicated to your source which created you. Make every action like there is no other option that you achieve your goals. Do everything in a great way and you will find that your beliefs make you unstoppable.

## *How to strengthen your belief*

The first step is to stop listening to negative media. All this negative energy from news will not bring you happiness or bring you close to your goal. It is important to know that in news there are only bad things, even not the most important. It is because most people like to listen about negative things and media will bring them this information, it is their work unfortunately. Stay in touch with what is going on but do not infuse your mind with this. Limit yourself to how much time you will spend watching, reading or listening to it.

Stop talking to negative people. Why? Because they are a negative ☺ Community of people around you which will form your values and beliefs. Hang around with positive people who are getting much better results than you are. They will infect you with positive vibration and strengthen your belief system. Then your mind will make habits that you seek.

Listen to personal development programs repeatedly. Absolutely obsess with these programs. Listen while you are working, even if you do not have a full concentration. Have them playing subliminally because your subconscious mind will be receiving benefit through the power of autosuggestion.

Repetition is the first law of learning on any subject. When you listen to these programs over and over again you will see that every time you learn new things. When you read it, hear it and affirm it you form your beliefs through the subconscious mind. That is exactly how you can change your beliefs to be positive. Affirm them, speak them, write about them, and you will be living them.

You can read a lie over and over and eventually believe it. This is the power of autosuggestion and I will explain it further in a moment.

## *Your Self Talk*

Your internal conversations are what you have in your own mind and are what constitute your self-talk.

Everyone talks to themselves; even if some people do not want to admit that. We are constantly having a conversation with ourselves. There is nothing wrong with that. In fact you can use this to put yourself in to a better position.

Be aware of your self-talk throughout your day. When something wrong happens to you, how do you react? Out loud or silently in your mind? When you receive a compliment do you reject this because you do not think you deserve it or you appreciate it and affirm it silently? These are powerful things to do.

If your self talk is negative, it will de-power you, drain your energy and finally there is a tendency to give up. Usually we have a tendency to think negatively about ourselves. What I am revealing to you right now has the power to completely transform your life and instantly makes you feel better about yourself.

If your self talk is positive, it will empower you. If you constantly affirm that you are a great person, you are a great partner, a great business owner you will just feel better throughout the whole day. When you do something wrong, don't beat yourself up about it. Better to say this: <u>*That's not like me*</u>, completely separate yourself from this action and you will rarely partake in it again.

Your self-talk builds your beliefs in a progressive way or it can draw you down. You know that you become what you think about and paying attention to your self talk is a great way to be aware of what you think about all day.

Your self talk identifies what your beliefs are. If you find your self-talk in a negative way, then you know that you have some beliefs to change. Immediately you will feel bad, so the best way to change your self-talk is to say and think the exact opposite. God, Creator or Universe whatever you call it, talks to you all the time. And he talks to you through your own voice. When you learn to listen and believe your own voice, whatever you do, you will be successful.

## *The power of Affirmations*

Positive statements to yourself, from yourself is what an affirmation is. You want to affirm things that you want to have or experience in the future. If you want wealth in your life you would make and affirmation regarding how wealthy you are. Even if the wealth is not around you now, create an affirmation that it really is. Similar like this: "I am bursting with Joy, Gratitude, Harmony and Money!" and say it over and over and over again. When you become what you think about, this is the best way to be what you desire to be. It can be used in any other area, like health, love and relationships. So make an affirmation and think about it all the time. Say it, feel it and believe that you are in such a state of being.

Repeated self-talk in the form of affirmation tells your mind what you want to be thinking about. It is a good way to direct your thinking. Again, you become what you think about.

The purpose of an affirmation is to take control of your self talk and of your consciousness. We are the only creatures on the planet that are aware of what we think about. You can direct very powerful energy in the form of mind and if you master this energy it will manifest whatever you desire.

You become what you think about. This is worthy to repeat over and over and over again. So make an affirmation that states exactly how you want to live and think on it OVER and OVER and OVER again.

Have it start with "I AM". I AM are two very powerful words which identifies your state of being. As soon you say those words unlimited energy flows right into your consciousness and when it first enters into your mind – it has no form. Whatever you say after that is the form that energy is going to take. Be aware what continues after I AM when you say this and say exactly in what state of being you want to be. We are constantly making I AM statements all day. I AM tired, I AM sick, I AM really excited for the party tonight. When you pay attention to your I AM statements you will be aware that they are in perfect alignment with your present results.

It should emotionally appeal because when you put emotion into this your action will be very effective. Every action in a negative state of mind is very ineffective so be positive when you say your affirmation, *feel it*. The more you feel the more great results you get.

Use present tense when you are affirming. Not I WILL, or SOMEDAY, EVENTUALLY – I AM. Feel like they have already happened. Your mind and the universe respond to your being, not to your wishing.

## *Take Action*

Make a goal card. A goal card is a small piece of paper that you carry with you all the time. It has affirmation written on it and you should read it as often as you can through your day. This is a constant reminder of your desire.

Post your goals up where you will see them often.

Environment is more important than heredity – you must surround yourself with the right people and especially when you are entering into an online business. In Carbon Copy Pro we are literally a family. We help each other and Jay setup a multi-tiered support system that both gets support to those who need help as well as gives leaders opportunity and experience to truly go out and create massive success.

Again, get around the right people – contact me today and I can introduce you to our family – Think of it as a support group for goal achievers.

# Your First Step To Living With Purpose

## *Purpose Explained*

Purpose, to me, means knowing what brings you the most love in life. It is when you do something that you do with love, not that you "have to do" or "should do", but because you want to. Same as love, when you love, you do because you want and it gives pleasure. How many times have you heard that love is not the end point, love is the way? When you know your purpose you act with love and this brings you happiness in to your life. Act with love and everything will follow.

It is also doing what you love the most in every area of your life. Do not think only about work, I mean every single area of your life. What do you love to do for recreation? What kind of activity do you love? What do you love to do with your family? – do that which brings you the most love and forget the rest. Forget about what everyone else will say about you.

Your Purpose is your *why statement.* This is very important. You must know why you are doing what it is that you are doing. This will bring you strength, which you need, on the way to your purpose. You should know that every way has obstacles and you want to beat them, not crash into them and then turn back. You want to know how to solve the problems not complain about them. When you have a strong *why* it is like a piece in your armor on your way when it is dark. There will be points during your walk when you will question your actions. There will be times when you are wondering why you just don´t play it safe and there will be days when you are filled with doubt. You should know that sometimes you experience this and in these times you realize how it is important to have a strong and clear purpose. It brings you back to your way and shelters you from loneliness and frustration.

If you have no defined purpose, you will have no true and lasting happiness. After all do you want to have a life without purpose? When you live life with YOUR purpose your life will be full of joy and happiness. If you lack a purpose you really do not have a reason to get out of bed in the morning. On the other hand, when you live with purpose sometimes you don´t want to sleep at all ☺.

## *Vision Explained*

A vision is a clear mental picture of future results you want to experience in every single area of your life. Vision shows you a direction of your activities. It is something you know about your future. As you create your vision, the universe will help you define it and clarify it. Do not be confused if that now you do not have a clear vision yet. Your vision will build and grow as you continue to define it. Do not wait for a vision to come to you all of sudden, start now to build your vision.

This is your ultimate reality. This is what you want. Just imagine you living the life of your dreams. Feel it! Do not let others influence you that this kind of life is for someone who has the destiny to live the lifestyle that you desire. YOU create your own destiny. You can have whatever you want. Remember that. See yourself in every single detail, feel the feelings of how that would feel and you will be amazed at how this vision of yours will come to live in your mind, then ultimately in your life, because you are becoming what you think about.

A vision is your *what*. You must know what you are doing and why you are going to do it. Vision is what you are doing and purpose is why you are doing it. Every time it is first why and then what. Before every action you should know why you are doing this, because your vision comes to mind and every act you do will be full of power and this act will be very effective.

Your vision is your roadmap to fulfilling your purpose. It gives you direction and a future to hope for. Hope is a fundamental element that we must always have in our life, and we don´t clearly realize it until we have lost it at some time.

Your vision is your biggest motivator in every action you do. Your motivation is your biggest friend and this friend will wake up you every single morning and help you to get out from you COMFORT ZONE. Your Comfort zone will not bring you happiness. Progress will bring you happiness. When you have a vision do not forget that you should have an element of urgency and this you will build by setting up BIG goals.

## *Goals Explained*

Goals are short-term steps that will lead you to your vision. They are stepping stones and sequential levels of life that will help you plot your course and still you know that you are on the right track.

Goals give your life direction and urgency. Every goal should have a timeline because without a timeline you can wake up years later with nothing but the same list of goals. Put urgency to your vision by setting some definite goals with time limits.

Goals give you focus and clarity as to what you must be doing TODAY. It is easy to get excited about big goals without any action oriented for today. Everything that can be done today, do TODAY. Wallace D. Wattles in his book named "The Science of Getting Rich" said: "If there is something that may be done today, and you do not do it, you failed in so far as that thing is concerned; and the consequences may be more disastrous that you imagine. Do not spend any time day dreaming or castle building; hold to the one vision of what you want and act NOW." Every day can be successful and when you have successful days you will live a successful life.

Goals give your potential direction to work towards and will play an enormous role in forming your daily habits. Vision tells you where you are going and habits get you there. Vision with no goal and action is nothing. Set up goals and act now.

## *How to Discover Your Purpose*

Start by journaling the things, people or events that inspire you or brings you tears of inspiration and your purpose will be formed by the time you journal them. As you grow you will get new ideas, new desires, new goals and new visions. Remember this: THE UNIVERSE IS FRIENDLY TO YOU – NOT AGAINST YOU. The Universe, Our Creator, or God wants to give you what will elevate your life and your life can elevate only your purpose, passion to do what you love. Never forget that the universe is friendly to you – NEVER.

Your inspiration leads you to your purpose and to the life you want. Have you ever wondered why some people, events, labor or ideas give you so much energy and inspiration? Have you ever wondered why that happens? That is this universe leading you down your path – it gives you a sign. Most people are walking around wondering why their life is not going the way they want it to and they are so absorbed in their circumstances that they do not see all the signs, that the universe is giving them what will lead them to their happiness. There are absolutely no coincidences, no accidents. Every single thing happens for an exact reason and that reason is to move you closer to fulfilling your purpose.

Give yourself plenty of time. It takes some time, nothing happens immediately. Do not push it by the force. Let it happen.

Your purpose can change at different points in your life. Nothing in this world is steady. As your body changes, your goals, visions and purpose will change, because your life will have different seasons and each different season will have a different purpose. Remember, your purpose is never something that you HAVE to do. It is never something that you MUST do. Purpose is full with love and joy. I think that it is worth to find your purpose don´t you think?

## *How to Create a Vision*

You start by asking yourself powerful questions. Powerful questions create powerful answers. You will experience that whatever question you have, already has an answer. Even the biggest and most complicated questions have answers. Sometime the most complicated questions have the simplest answers. Again ask yourself questions.

If my success were guaranteed, I would…that is the powerful question to ask. Think this way always; do not admit any possibility of failure. These questions give you motivation and will loosen the limits of your thinking and open your mind up to new ideas and possibilities.

If I knew I couldn't fail, I would…- answer this question. You will not know the answer right away, but if you keep asking, the answer will come. They will come sometimes in unexpected situations, but these answers are powerful and you will get a wave of new ideas and concepts that you were missing before.

The next step is to make a vision board. A vision board is a posting of all the things you want to be, do or have in your life. This puts your vision in picture form. It brings pictures to your mind and then to your life. If you have never created this before, send me an email and we can do it together.

Emotional appeal is the most critical factor because when you put emotions to your vision, things will manifest so much faster. Emotions are like water for the plant, without water the plant will die even if it has the best place to grow, the best gardener. Without water the plant will die. The same is with your vision, without emotion it will be very difficult to achieve something at all. Emotions run the entire universe and they are not something that should be taken lightly. Put your emotions in to a vision and you will see the results very soon.

You must have clarity about what you want. Nothing great happens without clarity. Sit down and get completely clear of what you want to do and have in your life. Make a plan of action as to the first step for them. Get absolutely clear.

## *How to Begin Setting Goals*

Make a list and prioritize the list. You know that nothing happens immediately and you will never have everything that you want in one day. In fact in such a case there will be no fun☺. Take time with this. Decide which goal is most important to you right now in this point of your life. The goal should be attainable, short term and have a realistic timeline. Set a great short term goal that will give you an early win and build confidence in yourself.

# The More You Give, the More You Get

## *The Law of Receiving*

The law of receiving states: in order to receive, you must first give before you get. Unfortunately many people think in reverse. There might be a thought in your mind that you have to have something at first before you give. The fact is that I just stated previously, you are SPIRITUAL BEING with INFINITE potential, which means that you are bottomless fountain of knowledge and bliss. You have everything that you need to start giving, but by reading this chapter of my book you will have more understanding of what it means.

You can give through many different avenues and many different ways. It is important to understand that giving in one form is not better than the other. Giving is giving and it could be as simple as opening the door for someone, or giving a smile to a total stranger. I have a friend who smiles to anybody and I've got to tell you, he is naturally a friend with everyone. When you give from your heart it is worth that as if giving a $5,000 check. There is absolutely no difference.

Give more to receive more and in that order. Again do not get hung up only on the money subject here. Forget about the very popular thought "I do not have enough money to do…" As soon as you do that you will open a gate in your mind to enormous possibilities. Of course money can play a role in the giving process, but it is not only means to express opulence and sometimes a simple smile gives more inner joy and satisfaction.

Look for opportunities to give absolutely everywhere you go to everyone. Try to give in any form, like a smile, holding the door or even giving them a hug. You will be surprised at how good it makes them feel and how you feel. My friends call it a *free hug*. As you focus your mind on giving, your mind will find out in any circumstances the possibility to give, or serve. The more ways you find the more money will flow to you, because money is the results of service and when you have good service you give a lot.

Make giving a habit, because giving and receiving is a beautiful cycle where you give and receive and give and receive to enormous degree.

## *Sowing and Reaping*

Sowing means planting "seeds" of service and helping others. The sow season is simply a season of sowing and after this comes the season of reaping. There is no other way. You have to at first sow and then reap. You cannot do it together and you cannot plant seeds and harvest next day, seeds need time before it is possible to harvest them. The only thing you can do is to make sure you are planting seeds of service each and every day to as many people as possible.

Reaping means collecting the fruits of your labor and enjoying the benefits of it. The more you seed the more you will reap, this is an inescapable law, who many people forget and they are very surprised that sometimes there is nothing to reap. Just like any of the laws of the universe you should use this law for your benefit.

You can do both in many different ways, as I stated earlier when your mind is focused on serving – giving- you find out uncountable ways and opportunities to do this beautiful activity and you will see the results. There is no doubt about it.

Sow the best service of which you are capable each and every day. Do and give the best and you will receive the best.

Sow into people's lives as much positive things as you can, to family, friends or even to a complete stranger. You may not be a relative but in spiritual meaning, we all are.

Love everyone unconditionally and try to give without expecting what you get. This is unconditional love. Just like a mother loves her child, whatever it takes. She does not serve him because she expects that she will get something back, she serves him because her love is UNCONDITIONAL. Make it a habit and you will shine, literally, with joy as you move throughout your day.

Sowing and reaping are two different seasons that happen at different times and if you are not confused with that, you will be able to collect the fruits of your labor very soon. Most people plant a seed of service and expect an instant return, but nothing happens and usually they finally give up. It is just like when you are digging the seed because nothing happened. You will destroy the seed and have to sow again. It does not work this way. You have to wait some time, this is worth repeating and repeating again.

There is a difference between giving and trading so do not twist these two words. Really try to give without expecting, because we all are conditioned to trade and if you expect something you do not give but trade. Just give, what you can and where you can.

Always be sowing because when you have INFINITE potential you do not need to worry that someday there will be nothing to give. For sure you will have a constant stream of good pouring energy over your sowing each and every day. This way, your life will be a beautiful trip, because goodness and mercy will follow you all the days of your life.

Always be extending your service that you provide. This sounds like commitment and maybe difficult to accept but as soon as you do this you will taste the nectar of serving others. There is no better reward when someone will thank you that thanks to you his/her life is better. And again money is only the results of service. The better service you provide, the more money you will get. So ask yourself the most important question in business and life: "How can I extend the service I render to my customers, neighbors, community and world"?

Always have new and better services to offer. In fact this is really challenging but you will be amazed of the constant inflow of ideas by asking powerful questions. For any question you have, you already an answer. Every successful person is asking them self important questions on a daily basis. As soon as you don't have any ideas, it is a sign that you stopped asking questions – it's as simple as that. Never ask yourself "Why can´t I…?", but ask, "How can I…?" You will see that your mind will reflect and act in a very different way.

## *Nothing Happens By Chance*

This is an irrefutable law, which is subtle, and we cannot see him by our own eyes, but we can see the results. Unfortunately we are conditioned that what we cannot see, we just do not believe.

Universal laws always work and again we can see only the RESULTS. For example, you cannot see the wind but you see how trees and flags billow according to the wind. The same with these laws we are talking about in this book, you cannot see them but you see the results in your life. Just be in harmony with them, do not fight with them and your life will be perfect.

Gravity is a universal law and everything in this universe is subjected to the law of gravity.

Throw a pen straight into the air and it always comes down, right? You never see the pen float in the air and after a while come back down. It always works. The same way with what you put out will come back to you. Remember when I was talking that energy always comes to the source? The more you give, the more you receive.

Luck is for people who let life happen to them, but people who want to direct their life they create luck for themselves. They create their own stories. Bob Proctor said that many people are an extra in their own story. Sometimes people said that "he is lucky", but they do not see the effort of the man who is successful. They only see the results so they think that the guy is just lucky. Nothing happens by chance. Have you ever seen a big company that was based on chance? Every time there is a sustained effort of people behind it.

Be a success by law, not by luck and when you know and act upon this fact, you will be much more motivated, right? How many people will start some business when they only expect that by chance luck will come to them? How much are sure that luck comes to you? You cannot base your life on waiting for luck; create your own luck by the laws of success, then your dream life will move towards you. Earl Nightingale, the Dean of personal growth said as you move toward your goal, your goal will move towards you. What a wonderful statement and one filled with truth and freedom.

## *Exchange an Abundance*

Give an abundance of yourself to receive abundance. Remember there is no limited supply for everyone. This make me think of the ancient scriptures called Upanishads where it is stated, *"From abundance, he took abundance and still abundance remained"*. Make every transaction, relationship and conversation with the intention of exchanging abundance. The more abundance you give, the more you will automatically receive in return and then will come the very important experience. You can call it realization, because you realize this law and you will see the results in your own life. No matter how small. This will give you inspiration and motivation to give more and more and your belief will be stronger. That is how you pick up your momentum and your expectation will SKYROCKET!

If you give life your best, life will give you the best. Just be in love with life and life will love you right back. As you sustain this state of being you will be surrounded with people, circumstances and events that reflect your state of being. State of being attracts similar things and when you read this book you know that this book was attracted by you. Again, anything like chance does not exist.

Do all the tasks in a great way because every act, even the small is playing an important role in the completion of the whole plan that you have, more than you think. Do every act with focus on your goal.

Constantly improve every single day even if it is only a 1% improvement per day and you will feel good and you will be amazed at the end result. 1% improvement every single day is a 365% improvement in a year. What would your income be if you increased it by 365%. It sounds good right?

The best way to give is to give of yourself. Every person has talents for something. Give your most natural talents to others in form of service and try not to think that you will get something. Any business is possible to do in a different way and you will be more effective if you will act in harmony with your talents.

## *What Do You Have To Give?*

Good. Now you know that you do not need any money to begin to give abundance. Money is only one means of opulence. Just be yourself and be prepared to give and you will find out that you can give opulence in form of attitude, enthusiasm and vibration and so forth. This is a place to start.

If you have a little money and still you want to give, GREAT. When you have $5 to give, find organizations that can take your $5 and turn it into food for people, or even clean water. If you can find one, start.

The good can take a while, but it will return. Maybe you do not see the results immediately, but wait for a while. This is something you must experience to believe and you will only believe through experience.

Stay focused on giving and serving to others. As you focus on giving and serving money will flow to you in endless avalanches of abundance.

# How To Choose The Right Business

*Your Plan B*

Plan B is an income backup plan or secondary stream of income that gives you and your family more support regarding the necessities for life. But we do not want to work only for surviving right? So this income can be your first step to having a more opulent life.

You can earn your living full time and build your fortune part time. You may not be in position to leave your job and start making it full time in your business, so start earning a second income until your necessities will be taken care of is a very good idea. There is nothing wrong with starting this way and home-based business can be a perfect place. This way you can build your full time income with ease without worries and anxiety if you can take care of your family.

J.O.B.'s have no security, the only security you have is within. Many people depend on outside circumstances and they think that they are secure until the company where they work gets into trouble, fires them, stops paying them health care or something like that. Again there is no security in a job, because you depend on someone who pays you so you have to be sure that you can take care of yourself. There is no potential or security outside of you. The only security and potential is within.

## *Evaluating an Opportunity*

Decision making is a skill that you want to definitely have, because making quick decision can be very relative to your capacity to produce a large income for yourself. Every wealthy and successful person has it. They want something; they make decision and remain committed to the end.

You will be bombarded with opportunities and information as you begin to look for some income opportunities and home based businesses to join. This can be very overwhelming which is exactly why I am writing this book to you instead of just explain everything about my business to you. I am here to help you and guide you through the decision making process.

**Company:** You must look for a solid company that has the right leadership in place with a good "track record" of past success. Look for a solid company with a great team of leaders and look for success stories. Email me right now and I will send you a lot of video testimonials from our members.

**Industry:** The industry must be something that is "hot" right now and has a major growth potential in the near and distant future. You must have an industry that keeps up and stays ahead of current market trends. Many companies are selling a product that were wonderful 10 years ago and that's why all of their distributors and members are broke.

**Products:** Your product must have four key elements: High impact, high commission, high volume and residual income. I strongly recommend you to find a product line that has both low price point products as well as high price point products. This is important so you can have constant small sales for you and your team as well as large commissioned sales that create excitement and momentum. You also must look for some kind of residual product in order to insure residual income for you and your downline.

**Potential Market:** Who can you sell your product to? Find a potential market of customers who will be looking for your product, have a tremendous immediate need for the product and who are willing to pay you for it.

**Compensation Plan:** The compensation plan is very important piece of this puzzle. I want to say again: You must have high impact and high commissioned packages in order to create excitement and great success stories. Make sure there is a way for long-term residual income, as well as, an outstanding way for a new person to enter into the business and earn money right away.

**Training and Support:** No matter how great the product, potential market, or company is there must be a proper support structure in place so everyone gets taken care of. You should be able to send in a support inquiry and receive a response in as little as a few hours. At the max your support ticket should be answered in less than 36 hours. Our company is very committed to helping and supporting all of our people. We do not see you as another distributor, we do not see you as a new recruit on our downline, we see you as a person who has a desire for something more – as a person who has goals and dreams – as someone with family, friends or causes you want to support and it is with that attitude that we work with and support all our people.

**Your Sponsor:** After you have observed and researched all the above mentioned topics, it is time to select the right sponsor for you. It is important for you to work with someone who resonates with your values, purposes and overall mission in life. When two or more people work in harmony in an opportunity, magic happens. However our support and training is such a quality, that you even do not need to have a great sponsor because with our training everyone is getting taken care of. It is great for new people, because they can make a lot of money due to our support center with business coaches who answer all questions of our potential customers. So if you are considering joining our company, you do not need to worry that if you are not a great sponsor you will not make any money.

## *The Industry*

We are in the fastest growing industry on the planet – internet marketing. This is the biggest, fastest growing game in the business world.

The internet is changing the entire game of business. Today the Internet is the best place to start a business and this is the opportunity to seize the moment and take action.

The internet is a teenager; it is only going to get bigger and better. The internet is only about 16 or so year old. This is just the beginning; there is no doubt about the great future.

No experience is necessary because you will learn the latest and greatest available steps. Our company is bringing the best available in the world today to teach you internet marketing, affiliate marketing, opportunity marketing, sales, money management as well as the cutting edge of personal development coaching with global leaders in the industry.

All that matters is your willingness to be coached and your desire to succeed. If you are willing, I will help you to become able.

## *The Product*

Our business is our product and our product is our business. Many people come to us simply for the product and many people come to promote the business and many people come for both, because we literally have the outstanding product, service and the support. We are the household name in the industry.

We get taught online marketing training, mindset training and income multiplication coaching. These are three elements to have a great business and LIFE.

Learn it once, apply it for a lifetime. Once you understand your unlimited potential you will be able to achieve any goal you set. This is what we teach in our school. Learn, understand and apply this knowledge every day for a lifetime. We take the success of our students, members and friends personally. Again we want to create success stories.

The need is enormous and it is only getting bigger. More and more people come to network marketing, online marketing and the home based business industry every single day. That will not change at all. Everyone needs to know how to do Internet Marketing correctly and have a mindset of an entrepreneur. Without these two things no one can ever succeed with online business. Nothing does this better than our Carbon Copy Pro.

People are looking for income opportunities more than ever and you can be the one who will help them. You can be in the gold rush right now. Now is the time for this industry. These people need help, they need to get knowledge, and they need to get training. Let´s help these people together.

## *The Potential Market*

Anyone willing to listen, anyone who wants a better life for themselves but they must be willing to fight on in the face of discouragement. We reach out to all people wanting more from their life and invite them to come as they are and join our revolution.

Our market is anyone looking for a better lifestyle and who want to help others. We do not have the mentality of just getting bills paid. We want to help as many people that we can and not only in the business. If you have enough for yourself you can take care of many others and make a better world.

We can get you more time. The one thing you cannot get back and the most critical asset of your life.

We can get you more money, because when you do not have to worry about money you will be amazed how much free time you have. And when you have this, the only thing you can do is to be more AWARE of YOURSELF and we give you that as well.

We deliver the best training on the web, with more time, money and knowledge you are unstoppable towards any goal you choose in your life.

## *The Compensation Plan*

You get paid very nicely. We have a multi-tiered compensation plan that pays big commissions and residual commissions to all. Our company wants to pay a REALY HUGE AMOUNT OF COMMISSIONS and if you want to have a piece of that, you must contact me immediately before all the spots are filled.

## *Training and Support*

We teach you everything you need to know. But there is the deal – we give you the knowledge as to exactly what to do, but also the awareness to act on the knowledge you have. Many people know what to do to get better results, but they still do not do it. They do not take consistent actions that they know will produce results. This is what we will help you understand and change.

Our training teaches you exactly what to do in a live, step-by-step manner. You will have a day's full of plans and actions.

Our training also teaches you why you do what you do and why not to do some of the things you would like to do. Because if all we needed to know was HOW to do something then everyone would be happy, healthy, skinny and rich. There is more to the puzzle than just know HOW to do something and that is what we provide for you.

# Money Chapter

## *What Money Actually Is*

Money is a green piece of paper, nothing more and nothing less. Money is a medium of exchange. It is for your benefit. If we think of money as a big, frustrating, difficult aspect of our lives, then money will be a source of frustration for us. Remember that you become what you think about? It applies also to the subject of money.

Money is not your master; you are the master of money but most cultures think in reverse. Unfortunately they let money run their lives. They let the amount of money they have in their bank account determine what vacations they will take, the house they will live in and the dreams they will pursue. This is not how it was intended to be. You first decide what you want and how you want to live and then you can determine how you can go about earning the amount of money you will need to afford the lifestyle you have decided upon.

Never let a green piece of paper stand between you and that which you want. Never let something like money stand in the way between you and the life of your dreams. If you have a big beautiful idea nothing like a green piece of paper can stop you. Again NEVER – EVER let money direct your life. You are the master of money and you direct and choose what happens in your life. If money is necessary to achieve your dream life than let´s earn some ☺

Before money, people used to barter services, products and animals as a medium of exchange. Meaning if I wanted some potatoes but I only had a cow, then I would have to find someone who had enough potatoes that was willing to exchange for and needed a cow. This was not only difficult but it is hard to negotiate assets such as these in exchange for one another. This is why money was created, to make exchanges easier and more frequent.

Money is a medium of exchange for goods or services between two or more parties. Money is not something that if one has them is lucky or that one is a better person.

Money is an exchange for services rendered. If you have a great service you will earn more money. If you want to earn more money, simply figure it out how to provide more and better service. More service = more money. It is just that easy.

Everything starts with how you think and there is no difference with money. How much money you will earn is determined first by how you think. Do not think about debt, focus on abundance. If you are focusing on debt, you will get more debt and it does not matter if you think about how to get out or get in. It is impossible to think how to improve your service if you are thinking about debt all day long. It is like trying to create a fire while it is raining. It simply will not work.

Everyone has the same amount of time and potential every day. Yet some people work 40 hours a week and earn around $2,000 while others work 20 hours a week and earn $20,000. Why is this? It is a mystery right? Because I know a lot of people who are very dedicated to their job and they work very hard, but they do not earn a lot. Why is this? I will explain this in details as you keep reading. Stop trying to work harder and work smarter is the first point of awareness you want to move into. Maybe you heard this before and it is really true. A person who earns $20,000 is highly creative, highly leveraged and has a completely different thought process than the person who is earning $2,000 per week. It absolutely does not mean one person is better than the other – that does not have anything to do with it and it is does not mean that person is smarter, he just knows something what the other does not. Keep reading and you will see it in a moment.

## *Money is Not Bad*

Money is not bad; the love of money is bad. I have heard that money is the root of all evil, but to be exact the love of money and evil itself is the root of all evil. Money cannot be the root of nothing, it is just a piece of green paper remember? Money is simply a tool. It can be used for an enormous amount of good and it can be used for an enormous amount of bad. It only depends on the person who has the money in their possession. You have a free will and you will choose what you are going to do with that.

Your life can be filled with purpose and money at the same time. If you are a good person and you earn a large amount of money you will be able to do a large amount of good. This is exactly why I want to help you become wealthy in every single area of your life - money included.
Good people use money for incredibly good things and so can you! Imagine that thousands of hungry children in Africa will get clothes and food thanks to you!!! WOW, isn´t that nice? Money is your till to create anything you want, and I know you will use it for good.

Money is just as important as the mortgage, food and education it buys. Money will never make you happy, but you must have it to operate in a civilized society. Wallace D. Wattles said: "No man can rise to his greatest possible height talent or soul development unless he has plenty of money, for to unfold the soul and develop talent he must have many things to use, and he cannot have these things unless he has money to buy them with."

If someone says that money is not important to them, they more than likely do not have any. I remember that I always said it. I always said money was not important to me so I did not budget my income, I did not manage it properly, because money was not important to me. Thus I did not have any of it.

Anything in life, that you say it is not important to you does not stay long. Imagine if you told your significant other that they were not important to you – would they stay around very long? If having a nice house is not important to you, you will not have one. The only things that we have in abundance are the things we value. When you value money, you will budget and save it, when you save it you will able to invest it, when you invest it you will be able to spread the seeds of your earnings to anyone and make good and help people.

## *Money and Happiness*

Money was not meant to make you happy. Anything like green piece of paper cannot make you happy. The only thing that makes you happy is your awareness, progress and decision. Being rich will not make you happy and neither will being in poverty.

Happiness is not in a bank account; happiness is not in a big house, in a sports car or in a perfect haircut. The only source of happiness is inside of you, in other words in YOU. Only you can make yourself really happy and only you decide if you will be happy or sad. We choose to be grateful or to be bored. It is our choice. Isn't it great that you can choose those things?

Money will not make you happy and poverty will not make you happy either ☺! It is all about what kind of lifestyle you are willing to earn.

Empty plates do not feed hungry individuals and you can be the one who will fill these plates. Isn't it awesome? Really give yourself a strong WHY that goes far beyond you. Your life will transform when you lose yourself in the service to others. Then money will never be a problem.

The source of happiness is awareness. Awareness, that you are the source of your happiness. It is not anything outside of you. It is within and you can choose happiness!

The source of happiness is progress and I mean constant progress. The happiest people are those who every day are making progress towards the fulfillment of their individual purpose! Fulfilling your purpose is a beautiful and wonderful thing, even in the middle of a tragedy. In the tough times you really test your desire and love to do what you are doing and why you are doing it. When you have tough times you just keep moving forward to your purpose and then you realize that this brings you the most happiness. These are progresses that you make, even if you are not having the best day. Why – because you really test your love for what you do. You do it for love and this you realize only when you are tested. It is love and Love Never fails.

Happiness comes from being in alignment with your highest values and participating in the game of life. Life is just a game and you want to learn how to play and how to cooperate with other players because you are not the only one on this big playground. You want to be a team player and in a team, players help each other.

The source of earning large amounts of money is large amounts of services being rendered to a large amount of people. The more service you render the more money you earn. It is just that simple.

You must have highly specialized and intelligently applied knowledge for a specific area or "niche" you want to serve people in. Decide upon what you love doing and become a master that other people will willingly pay you to do it.

You can start today to earn more money by asking yourself how you can extend the service you are rendering to more people. Remember when I was talking that on every question you ask yourself you already have an answer? Contemplate as how you can increase the quality of service you are currently rendering to your current clientele. More service is always the answer.

## *The Law of Money*

The law of money states that the amount of money you earn will be in exact ratio to 4 things. This formula is as exact and unfailing as the law of gravity. It will work every time with every person. The amount of money you and I earn is in exact ratio to these four things:

**The need for what you do:** Is there a definite need for the services you are rendering? If you are trying to sell records to the masses today, you will be out of luck. There is no major demand for that product. There must be a need for what you are doing.

**Your ability to render your service:** This is the second and most important piece of this puzzle. You must be very good at rendering the service or selling the products. There must be a need for what you do and you must become very good at filling that need.

**The difficulty to replace you:** The better you get, the more difficult you will be to be replaced. No one is more valuable as a person, but some people have chosen to develop more skills than others.

**The quantity of the services/products delivered** is the last phase of this equation. If you are very good at providing service in some business, the only limit you will have is the quantity or volume of business you can handle. The more people you serve the more money you make.

Select something you love to do and begin mastering it. Master it, get amazing good at it and people will come from all over the world to be served by you.

Contact me as soon as possible and we can discuss what your passion is and how to turn it to opportunity. At least I can direct you to someone who can.

## *The Three Ways to Earn Money*

Trading time for money is the first and worst way to earn money. Almost everyone does it and it does not work very well for anyone.

Trading money for money is the second way you can earn money, but in this strategy you must have a lot of money to even begin with.

Leveraging your time and efforts through multiple sources of income is by far and away the best way to earn money and it is the easiest way to get started through the technology we have available to us today through the internet and home based industries!

The best strategy is to leverage yourself through multiple sources of income and that is what I am doing right now with my business. I am working from the comfort of my home, following in a proven system and it is a system that anyone can duplicate no matter where you are in your life.

# How to Brand Yourself

## *What is your brand?*

Your brand is essentially how you want the market to perceive you. What you want to be "known" for. Your brand is about who you are, what you do and why you do it.

This is a declaration of your values in business and what you are all about. Your brand will help you attract people who are on the same wavelength. You want to cooperate with people who are in harmony with what you do.

There are no major companies/individuals who do not have a brand. Every big company has a brand. Sony has a brand, Dell has a brand, and everyone knows what these companies do and what they offer. This is essential for their business.

No consistent brand, no consistent following, no consistent following, no consistent sales and that is what you want – consistency in all areas. This can be the most important document you read about your business because without a clear brand, you will never create anything of lasting value online.

## *Clarity*

The more clarity you have, the more concise your brand will be. Your brand has to be clear, because only then people will really know what your concern is and how you can help them. The more chaotic your brand the more chaotic the results you get. Success comes from order, failure comes from chaos. When you have clarity, you will commit to the success of your brand and you achieve something only if you are committed to it.

The more concise, the easier it will be to recognize and remember. No one can remember some quote that is three paragraphs long. Your brand is your direct statement to everyone who comes across you and it must be Bold, Attractive and Compelling.

Your clarity will equal your prospect quality. You will never help anyone else gain clarity unless you have clarity yourself. If you can´t get people "get it" when you are talking about your opportunity, it is because you don´t "get it" either. The more clarity you have, the more conviction you will possess and with conviction comes power to convince.

## *Passion*

Passion is an attracting emotion. When you are passionate about your opportunity you will naturally attract people who want to do something in their lives and they will also have passion. I think that you want to cooperate with passionate people right?

Without passion, you will have no enthusiasm and without enthusiasm there is no motivation to do something at all. You know that without action you will only dream about your goals. And who will get excited about you and your opportunity if you are not excited.

It is one of the most powerful emotional frequencies in existence. When you are passionate about something you put emotion into action and when you have in harmony your thoughts, feelings and actions you create an attitude. Attitude of course can be good or bad, but on this topic I write in my book so I will not analyze attitude here. The bottom line no passion, no persuasive power.

Passion causes you to go the extra mile. You need to go the extra mile every day and from passion arises invisible power that will help you when you need it the most. It will give you energy and direction; this all comes from your own personal passion on regards to your brand.

## *Purpose*

If you have no purpose, your brand will constantly change and when you constantly change your brand, you will never have a steady name on the market and people will not remember you. You will be easily swayed by other peoples opinions, economic times and excuses that are totally invalid, but easy to adopt. And this is what you do not want.

If you have no purpose, you have nothing and your brand will have no substance. Purpose and passion are what gives your brand meaning and a reason for people to want to join you. Make your purpose about something big and beautiful, something so enormous that it will take much more than your efforts alone to make it happen.

## *The craziest and most effective way to help build your brand*

Write your own obituary. Sounds crazy right? But when you do this it gives you insight into what you care about most, what you want people to think about you. Will this be uncomfortable, scary and even crazy – YES – and so is almost every critical successful behavior. If you are doing the same thing as the masses, you need to really sit down and rethink how you think, behave and live.

### *The Only questions you need to build your brand*

*What do you do?*
*Why do you do it?*
*Why should a prospect work with you?*

Work on these until your answers are one sentence in length. When they are one sentence length, break it down to three words. When you have done this, you have created your brand, you now have clarity and you can now move forward with passion and purpose! Remember – Life is a Game Enjoy it!

# The Laws of Success

## *Nothing Happens By Chance*

Luck is for people playing victim in life. When you believe in luck you also believe that everything happens by chance. The best thing you can do is to completely forget about luck once and for all. When you depend on luck all your work and effort can be useless because you miss the luck. If this was right, nobody would ever start some project or work. "Luck", you could say is created by all out massive action.

Banish luck from your vocabulary and from your mindset. As long as you believe in luck, you will not take full responsibility over your results and we want the exact opposite. Do not wait for luck, go and create your own luck.

Observe nature and you will see that nothing happens by luck or chance. Everything is working precisely according to the laws of nature.

There are over 7,000,000 species working in perfect harmony on this planet. It all operates perfectly and you are part of that perfection. Isn't that amazing that all planets and the universe is working according the laws and in perfect harmony? And you are a part of this divine nature, you are not separate.

Observe your own body and notice that every single cell in your body is working for a definite purpose and all the cells are working together. The body itself is one of the most magnificent instruments on the planet and you live in one. Be very grateful for that. Once you understand yourself you understand that everything in this universe is directed by laws.

If everything is subject to universal law, so is success. Just as every single thing in the psychical universe is subject to the law of gravity, so is every area of our life subject to the laws of success. When you understand how these laws works you can live in harmony with them. When you live in harmony every single area in your life will go along with success. You will be creating and live the life that you want to experience not to be waiting for "luck".

## *The Law of Cause and Effect*

The law of cause and effect states that what you put out into the world comes back to you every single time and in every single way. It works all the time, everywhere and for everyone.

Results are effects; you must understand the cause in order to change the effect. In order to change any effect, the cause must be changed. Now look at the area of your life where you are not completely satisfied with and ask yourself a question what is the CAUSE of that particular result. As you do this you become aware that you are completely in control of the cause, the cause within yourself.

Thoughts, feelings and actions are the cause of our results. All these three aspects together create our attitude. These three elements: Thoughts, feelings and actions are the most crucial pieces of your success. However when you master the first one (thoughts), you will automatically master the other two. Later you will see that our attitude is the main cause of our results.

Treat everyone you meet with love and respect and you will see that it will come back to you. Just love all of them, no matter what they say or what they do. When you love others you will be in love with yourself and if you are not in love with yourself you cannot love others. It is a natural cycle. The more you love others the more you will love yourself and the more the universe will love you right back. Love is always the correct answer.

Do only good to others and you will not only feel wonderful for doing it, but you will have some absolutely profound relationships. And what is life without relationships? Act kindly to others and you will find a great taste in doing it, because it is the most simple and basic principle of love, but only a few people do it. Become one of them and your life will be full of joy and happiness.

## *The Law of Attraction*

The law of attraction states that like attracts like. All things, people and circumstances in your life were – to a degree - attracted to you by your way of thinking. No matter if we are talking about bad things or good things. It works for both.

Like people are attracted to like people and you can see this around you. Have you ever seen wealthy people, who are hanging around someone who constantly complains and lives in poverty? Please understand correctly – it does not mean that one is a better person then the other, it has nothing to do with it, it is not the point. The point is that wealthy people hang around with wealthy people. They go to the same clubs, shops and vacation in the same places, like attracts like.

You attract what you are in harmony with and what are your most dominate thoughts. Be aware that you attract things to your life just by the way of thinking. Maybe it is a first time you are hearing this, but keep reading and you will see that the proof of this law is always around us.

What happens when you push a drop of oil and water together? Do they come together as one? Of course not, they repel. Why do they repel, because they are not in harmony with each other – like attracts like.

What happens when you push two drops of water together? They become one. The things you are in harmony with will come into your life just as sure as the two drops of water come together. It is really interesting right? Keep reading…

Start to observe the events in your life more closely. You will see when you study these things to some depth why some things and circumstances happen to you and you will be able to direct these things. Observe events and reflect on your experience and observations.

Change the way you think and feel because you attract everything in to your life the way of how you think and how you feel. From thoughts come feelings and from feelings comes a specific action which produces specific results, because you act according to your feelings. Everything begins with thought, so start to control what you think of all day. You can choose in any place and under any circumstance how you will think. It is your power to control your thoughts, so start today. You will see that the more you think about it and practice you can more and easily control your thoughts, then feelings and then actions. When you change the way you think, you will change and if you will change, everything will change for you. This is my favorite quote from Jim Rohn. Let me repeat it again: "If you will change, everything will change for you."

Build a mental picture of what you want, rather than what you do not want. Most people think about what they do not want and they are amazed why some things happen to them throughout their life. It is our condition to think more about things which we do not want. You will become what you think about so build a mental picture of what you want, rather than what you do not want.

## *The Law of Perpetual Energy*

This law states that energy is always moving into form and through form. The energy is never destroyed. Think about it for a while. You can see this also in nature, for example trees – Imagine a tree in the winter – the tree is bare right? What happens in the spring? The tree starts to bud…then the tree fully blooms and when the autumn comes the leaves fall off and the tree is bare again. This is a perfect example of energy moving into form and out of form.

Energy always manifests itself in every way. Maybe you think that we are really getting into some heavy stuff here, but again, just observe things around you and you will see proof of this everywhere.

Thoughts are energy, and they will manifest into psychical results in your life. Your thoughts are energy and according to what you are thinking, that energy will manifest in outwards results in your life.

You are a creation machine because as you think, you create. You can choose to think of whatever you want. There is of course some waiting period, because it will be not very cool if you think, for example elephant, and boom an elephant is standing right before you. But you can feel that creating process now; just feel about something really bad – do you feel the feelings that your body has? Do you feel those bad feelings and anxiety in your body? Things are happening right now. You are a creating machine and you constantly do this as you think, and you think all the time.

Every thought is a creation whether that thought is good or bad. It does not matter. I AM not good at this…I AM never going to figure this out…I AM sick..I AM I AM I AM…every single statement or affirmation is a creation.

Everything starts with *I Am.* Just like I said in one of the previous chapters I AM is a very powerful statement so be aware of what you think all day, what is your I AM statement. As you are aware of your I AM statements you will see that they are perfectly in match with your present results.

Pay very close attention to what you are thinking each and every day. This is so important that I can repeat it in every chapter. Pay as much attention to this as possible. You might be surprised by what you catch yourself thinking about most often.

Realize that everything starts in thought and as you think, you are creating. When you are aware of what you think, you choose your thoughts wisely, then your feeling will be in harmony with your thoughts, and then your actions will create results that you seek. This is so important. We can say that this is PRIMARY CAUSE OF YOUR RESULTS – everything is beginning with a thought.

## *The Law of Opposites*

This law states that everything in the universe has an opposite and I mean everything. You cannot have left without right, up without down, light without darkness. You cannot have the opposite without the other. Everything has the opposite and the opposites exist simultaneously.

This law guarantees that you will find what you are looking for. When you are in your town you can see the good things and you can see also the bad things of your town. It only matters what you pay attention to, which side you put your energy, good or bad. You can do this right now, think about your city where you live and try find out the good things about your city… As you think about the good things, you miss the bad things and this is how it works in reverse. They will be equally good and bad. If there is the same amount of good things and bad things – then that only leaves one conclusion… you will find what you are looking for.

If there are 1,000 reasons why you cannot do something, there are also 1,000 reasons why you can do that very thing. REMEMBER THIS – if you can think of million reasons as to why you cannot achieve your dream… that means, by absolute law, there must be one million reasons as to how you can achieve your dream… everything has opposite remember. It only matters which side you are giving your attention.

Write your goal down and only focus on all the reasons as to how you will reach your goal. There will be reasons that come into your mind with respect to why you cannot reach that goal, but disregard these reasons completely. Forget about them.

This will introduce you to your genius, just by thinking and only thinking about HOW YOU WILL reach that goal. Most people focus on the opposite side, this is our condition or habit, and your goal is to change your habit and become a person who acts in exact opposite. When you focus on WHY YOU CANNOT REASONS, you suppress you inner genius. Start to do it today and you will see the results first in your mind, then in your feelings and finally in your results.

You can literally do anything you can imagine in some way, shape or form. If you see yourself living the lifestyle of your dreams – YOU ARE ABLE TO LIVE THAT LIFESTYLE! You only have to become the person you need to become in order to create, attract and sustain that life. Stop focusing on only the doing and start by working on your BEING.

## *The Law of Rhythm*

Everything in this universe has a rhythm. We have a sun rise and the sun set. We see the rain come and the sun follow. The tide will come in and the tide will go back out.

Just observe nature and you will see the evidence. You will also see the perfection in this rhythm.

In order to experience growth, there must be rhythm in your life. There will be good times and bad times. You must have some rhythm or no growth occurs.

You will have good times and bad times, it is natural. The bad times happen, they are not fun, but that is when you learn the most about yourself, what you are doing and why you are doing it. There is no one who has achieved enormous success – and sustained it – who did not have a tremendous struggle either early or late in their life. You have to know that sometimes, bad times come otherwise you will be confused. When you know this, you will be prepared for these times and you will overcome them.

In times of bad swings, persistence will be required, the more you push forward in the bad times, the better the good times will be. You just keep moving forward and this will guarantee your success.

## *The Law of Relativity*

Nothing is good or bad, big or small until you relate it to something else. Only when you relate two or more objects then one stands out as small or large.

Everything is relative and so are your results. Your results are only bad when you relate them to someone else who is getting much better results. Your results are good relative to much poorer results. By using this law accurately, you will spark your being with tremendous gratitude.

No matter what we are going through, there is always someone else going through much worse. By comparing your results to something that is much worse, you can instantly spark yourself with gratitude and gratitude is one of the most beautiful emotions that you can experience.

Can you see, hear, walk, and talk? Do you have shelter and the basics of survival? Then you are living better than most people throughout the world. I am trying to be always grateful that I have a healthy body and that my senses work properly, because if I don't have good health, what the heck do I have? If I am not healthy I cannot do what I love. Be always grateful what you have got, there are many people who are in much worse conditions – remember that.

The best thing you can do is to remember all the things you are grateful for. Remember to do these things in the middle of your day. Refuse to get caught up in all the tasks and things of that day and choose to remember what you are grateful for no matter what.

Post reminders all around of these laws and of this one in particular. Gratitude is the most powerful emotion you can experience it – operate with it at all times.

## *The Law of Time*

Again, things cannot manifest instantly and this is a good thing because imagine that you think about lion and BOOM, right next to you a lion is standing in your living room. This would not be very pleasant.

Every goal is like planting a seed. Every seed takes a certain amount of time before it will manifest itself in full form. Every seed has an incubation period that must elapse and your goal is the same.

There is a definite gestation period required for the seed (goal) to fully manifest and your goal is a spiritual seed. You will not be able to tell how long it will take in order for your goal to fully manifest itself. All you know is that you must keep watering that seed, caring for it and working for it. The only way it will not manifest is if you give up on the seed.

## *Introduction to My Story*

When you're looking for opportunities on the Internet, you read countless stories about people who came to amazing wealth in a few hours by using their secret strategy. We have all read these amazing stories, but who believes them? I do not want to be another person who will tell you this story how I came to amazing riches, in fact I want you to know that I am going to be learning with you. I will not be in front of you as much I will be beside you.

The three main things I want to impress upon you are that I do not work with people who are not passionate about what they want and what they do. I also want you to know that I take my business very seriously while having fun at the same time. The three rules of my work are 1. *Be on purpose* 2. *Get results* 3. *Have fun*. That is how I work and this is the way I encourage everyone who works with me.

I want you to know I am a real person; I am not someone who is fictional. I am not an expert on everything, I am not the smartest person on the web, I am not the most successful entrepreneur in this industry, but I want you to know that I work hard, I want to help others as much as I can, if I make a mistake, I fix it, if I don't have an answer, I will find it for you.

I do not walk in front of you; I walk beside you in your path to growth and success. I am your partner in your business and your success truly is my success.

We can learn together and grow together. I build my business and relationships at the same time. When you decide to join me in business that is not the end of our relationship, it is the beginning of the beginning.

## *My Beginning*

I started looking for something more out of life when I was working in the office as a structural engineer and I was not satisfied with my present results and with my job. Later on I had tried the insurance business, but after a year I was not really successful – but now I know why. I was working hard, but still without the results that I expected. I had a desire, but without a proper mindset and action. I was working hard, but not smart. So I started looking for some other income opportunities and from that point I really decided to change my present results and every single aspect of my life for the better.

I knew I had to make some changes in my life when I realized that my income will not fulfill my desires to take care of my family, travel, buy a new car and new house and so on. I also wanted to change my attitude in every single area of my life. I wanted to change my view of the world and I did not know how I should do it, I only knew that it had to be done.

I also knew it was now or never and I just made the decision to change even though I was filled with doubt. I just started to move forward.

I looked for a while on the Internet for opportunities, because I was aware that when you start an online business you do not need to invest crazy amounts of money as in offline businesses. I also knew that an online business is the future of all businesses. While I was looking for some opportunities I had just read the book The Secret for the second time and I had a strong feeling that this industry was the right one for me. I did not know why but this feeling was so strong that it filled me with gratitude, passion and joy.

I did not know exactly how I would do it, but I just knew I had to do *something* and doing *something* is always better than doing nothing at all. So I kept looking and searching and growing.

## The Moment

Before Carbon Copy Pro I tried several opportunities, but I spent more money on advertising then I made. When I came across information about Carbon Copy Pro I was absolutely blown away. When I discovered that in this project you will learn how to do internet marketing properly and also learn about personal development I was so excited, because I knew that this is exactly what I needed and what I was looking for the whole time and that this would help me to reach my goals.

When I first looked into the information, I knew I had to learn more. So I attended webinars, read into websites and after this I joined immediately.

I shifted my thinking because I knew my goals were now possible no matter how impossible they seemed at the present moment.

I knew I had to take the first step even though many factors were still unknown. And step by step I started to work on my business.

Right after I made the decision, there was some fear simply due to the fact that I did not know all the facts that are necessary to achieve my goals.

Even though the fear was there, I kept taking small steps which turned into larger steps which turned into big strides. It is all about the following the proven steps. I knew that I needed to follow these steps and have a faith in the process.

## *The Company*

The biggest shift the company (Carbon Copy Pro) helped me make was to really start working on myself and be the person that I wanted to be. Because I had the right people around me, it was very easy to push myself and that is the most important – persistence.

This was a critical point in my business because I knew I was onto something HUGE! Almost every time when I started something I did not persist, but my vision and vision of Carbon Copy Pro helped me to persist. When I realized that I can have a business from home where I will help people and earn serious money at the same time my desire to be in Carbon Copy Pro was growing every day.

## *The Timing*

The timing was right for me to make a decision because there is always the right time to make a decision.

I knew the timing would never be perfect and I knew I had the idea to help others and I just decided to act. You can do it the exact same way.

There is never a good time for falling in love, having a baby or starting a business – that is just the way life is. There is never a perfect time for fresh ideas and new businesses. We have to simply try to turn our ideas into reality and make successful days, weeks, months and years.

The biggest factor that helped me make my decision was that I was looking for something like that; even though I was not aware that there was a vault that contained all that I needed to be successful in an online business. Personal growth and Internet marketing education combined all in one place. I must admit that I also knew that I attracted this project to myself, because I was really interested in the subjects that are in the book The Secret.

I still had fear the entire way, but the one thing I learned when I moved past my fear was that fear is just fear. As weird as it sounds, fear is just an emotion and it is an emotion ONLY. Fear is not real; it is my own self trying to hold me back from becoming something truly great. Fear is only fear; emotions are only emotions so I moved to all out massive action immediately!

# Decision Making

## *The Power of One*

What I mean by the power of One is the amount of impact a single decision can make upon many lives. Sometimes we might think that a decision does not have a big impact on our lives and the lives of others, but this is not true. Every single decision you make has an impact on your life and the lives of people around you. Usually the small decisions that we make every single day have the biggest impact on our overall life.

Henry Ford made a decision and everyone knows the results he created. He decided that he wanted to make automobiles available to anyone regardless of their social or financial status – he stuck on that decision and now everyone has a car.

Thomas Edison made a decision; he completely refused to quit when he was trying to invent the first light bulb and harness electricity. After over 10,000 failures he succeeded. Now everyone enjoys the benefits of the one man's decision.

You already make a big difference, even though you may not be fully aware of the impact you are having. We are all making big differences in many peoples lives – we just do not always realize it.

You can make a positive difference or a negative difference – the choice is yours to make with every action you take. Every time you choose, you impact others.

Your potential is unlimited and your impact is immeasurable. The only way to measure your impact is by telling stories, testimonials and memories. It is your time to make some new memories for your life and others as well.

Everyone has failed at some point in their life. You cannot have success without failure and you cannot have failure without success. Failure is an essential element to living a truly successful life. We have been conditioned to believe that it is a bad thing and it is not. Failure is essential because that is when you will learn the most.

Do not set tomorrows goals based on yesterdays failures. This is guaranteeing that tomorrow will be the same as today or yesterday. You can choose today that your life will be different and you can move forward to create the life you truly want to have.

## *Decision Making Creates Momentum*

Decision making is a skill of incalculable value and it is sad that we have not been taught this skill in pre-school. If you look at every successful person throughout history, that person was an outstanding decision maker. You must be able to make a decision if you want to succeed. The good news is that decision making is a skill and if it is a skill, it can be taught and learned.

We were never taught to make decisions in school, but this subject should be included in our education.

Decision making separates the leaders from the masses; there is absolutely no question about it. Many people want to be a BIG decision maker, but at the end of the day they do not want the responsibility that comes along with decision making.

Leaders who make a difference make decisions quickly and change them slowly, if they change them at all. Napoleon Hill wrote in his famous success book "Think and Grow Rich" an entire chapter about decision making. He stated that the ability to make decisions and to stick with that decision is one of the prime causes of success. Being that this is such a vital aspect to your overall life and success, lets talk about how to make decisions.

violate the right of others. If the answer for the last question is no, you do not move forward. If the answer is yes, you Take Action Now!

If all three answers are YES, you must move forward! This is your moment! This is your time to make things happen for you in a way that you never thought possible. When you move forward you automatically reach success. Forget about the past failures, it is in the past and that is where it will stay. When you move forward you have won the biggest battle of your live. The battle of trying! Many people never win this battle, because they are afraid to even try. Always know that the every action of moving forward is a success all in and of itself!

www.ingramcontent.com/pod-product-compliance
Lightning Source LLC
Chambersburg PA
CBHW081421080526
44589CB00016B/2625